My
Father's
Words

PATRICIA MacLACHLAN

My Father's Words

KATHERINE TEGEN BOOKS
An Imprint of HarperCollins Publishers

Katherine Tegen Books is an imprint of HarperCollins Publishers.

My Father's Words
Copyright © 2018 by Patricia MacLachlan

Library of Congress Control Number: 2018900201
ISBN 978-0-06-268769-2

Typography by Andrea Vandergrift
18 19 20 21 22   CG/LSCH   10 9 8 7 6 5 4 3 2 1

First Edition

In memory of Bob,

P. M.

With thanks to Bill.

CHAPTER 1

The Eternal Fitness
of Things

My father, Declan O'Brien, beloved shrink to many people, sings as he makes omelets for our breakfast.

My father is not fond of my word "shrink." He prefers "psychologist." But he is patient with me.

"Do you talk in your sessions?" I once asked him.

He smiled.

"We talk, or not," he said.

I'm not sure what that means, but one day I may know the meaning of his words.

He sings his favorite egg-making song, his favorite hiking song, his favorite basketball-playing song—called "Dona Nobis Pacem."

"Dona nobis pacem, pacem.
Dona nobis pacem."

My father's voice is sweet and he sings in tune.

The eggs will be too runny. He always makes them too runny, and he knows my younger brother, Finn, and I will slip them back into the frying pan until the eggs are hard. Finn once skimmed a stack of hard omelets across the backyard like Frisbees, evidence of his second-grade sense of humor.

"Passive aggressive?" I suggest to my father, who has taught me something about psychology.

I know passive aggressive means he might be doing the *nice* thing of cooking us eggs, while not making them the way we like.

My father is impressed. He smiles at me and shakes his head.

"It's the eternal fitness of things, Fiona," my father says, peering at me.

"He grew up with runny eggs," says Finn.

"How do you know that?" I ask.

"He tells me things," says Finn. "Because I ask him."

"What's that? The eternal fitness of things?" I ask my father.

His cell phone rings. Trouble calling.

I don't hear the answer to "the eternal fitness of things." Not then. Not ever from my father.

My father sets down the phone and puts on his jacket.

"Emergency," he says quickly. "Tell your mom when she gets home, Fiona. She's in class."

My mother is getting a degree in something undefined. Somewhere between philosophy, dance, and making brushed-wool dolls for preschoolers. She has been at it for two years, and my father has made his appointments around her schedule.

Once when Finn, my father, and I were playing basketball in the driveway, I made a joke of my mother studying early childhood.

"Kids are kids," I said.

My father did not smile. He was serious, and I knew it.

He grabbed the basketball from me.

"We can learn more from children than we sometimes learn from adults. They are open. No prejudgments. Your mother knows that."

He made a perfect jump shot into the basket.

"*Swish,*" he said happily. "Soon my jump shot will be as fine as your mother's."

I listened. And now when I look at little children, I think of my father's words. Children are wise, but they don't know how wise. And sometimes they don't have words for what they know.

My father hurries to the car and backs out of the driveway.

On the way to his clinic a truck driver hits him as my father swerves to avoid a child chasing a ball into the street.

* * *

By the time the phone call came, my father was dead.

"Dr. O'Brien died on impact, Mrs. O'Brien," said the doctor to me, thinking I was my mother. For some reason the phone was on speakerphone, so Finn heard what I heard.

I couldn't protect him.

"Mrs. O'Brien?" the doctor asked softly. He told me more details, but I stopped hearing.

I slowly hung up the phone.

Finn's face was very pale. Tears began to slip down his cheeks.

Without knowing what I was doing or why I was doing it, I took down two white plates.

I slipped the cold omelets onto the plates and put them on the table.

We began eating the runny omelets my father made for us. Neither Finn nor I talked. We just ate.

It seemed like the only thing to do.

Maybe it was the eternal fitness of things, whatever that is.

Our mother came in the door, so quietly that we didn't hear until she sat next to us at the table. Her jacket made a swishing sound against the chair. I thought of my father's words after his perfect jump shot into the basket.

"*Swish.*"

"The hospital called my cell phone," she said softly. "After they talked to you."

She looked thin and pale, like Finn, and deflated, as if the air had been swept out of her. It was quiet, strange with my mother in the room since she always laughed. My father smiled, but my mother laughed.

Across the table Finn straightened.

"It happened because he swerved the car so he wouldn't hit a child chasing a ball into the street," said Finn, startling us. It was the first time he'd spoken since the phone call.

"No one told me that," said my mother, her voice a whisper. "Of course he would do that."

"How could a mother allow her child to chase a ball into the street?" asked Finn loudly.

"How could a mother let this happen to

you?" said my mother, echoing Finn's words.

She looked at our plates.

"You're eating your father's runny eggs," she said.

And that was when she began to cry.

Finn and I put our arms around her then, and she seemed to grow into our mother, taking us both into her arms, growing larger and stronger again.

CHAPTER 2

Hero

My father's will said "no funeral." Included with the will was a note from him.

"Have a party!" it said in his handwriting. "Eat cake, drink champagne, and play basketball!"

"May I drink champagne?" asked Finn.

"No," said my mother.

She smiled. Maybe one day soon she'd laugh.

"At least I can eat and play basketball," said Finn.

"Yes. Basketball is good," said my mother.

She had a faraway look, and I knew she was thinking about the times she and my father played loud and competitive basketball games. It was embarrassing. Sometimes our neighbors Duke, Daisy, and their son, Luke, who was in my fifth-grade class, came out to watch as my parents called, "Out of my way, Claire!" and "Watch this, Dec!" loudly. My mother always made her three-pointers. Duke was amused. He wasn't competitive. But Daisy was a scrapper, taught by my mother. She once sank a

12

wild midcourt basket while facing away from the hoop. Duke just shook his head.

The party for my father was somehow both joyful and sad, with laughter and tears all mixed up. Finn and I were confused at that. My grandparents were ill and far away and couldn't come. My mother spoke to them every day on the phone. But cousins and aunts and uncles came. And friends.

My father's brother, Uncle Connor, came, looking so much like my father, it made my throat hurt. He put his arms around us, trying to be our father.

But he wasn't.

Luke came with Daisy and Duke. Luke sat between Finn and me, saying nothing. Luke didn't talk much ever, and that was one of the things I liked about him.

"I'm here," he said finally.

"I see that. Thanks."

Finn moved closer to Luke.

And we just sat.

People came and went. And at the very end of the day the doorbell rang.

"Would you get that?" my mother called to me.

I went to the door and saw a young man standing on the steps.

He looked familiar.

"Hello, Fiona," he said calmly. "I won't

come in, but I have a card for your family."

When I heard his voice, I remembered when I was very young and he had come to the house.

I'm four, and Thomas says hello to my mother and comes in the house. He carries a rug and a wastebasket and a guitar.

"I've come to move in for a while," he says.

My mother smiles.

"I'll call my husband," she says.

Thomas plays the guitar for me until my father comes and kindly helps Thomas carry his things back out to his car so he can live at his own house.

"No more guitar?" I ask my father sadly, beginning to cry.

My father hugs me.

"I'm sure he'll come again with his guitar," he says.

He was one of my father's favorite patients.

"Thomas?" I said.

"You remember."

He smiled and handed me the card. "Your father was my hero," he said. "I wrote that in the card."

He turned and walked back down the steps. My heart beat faster.

"He was my hero, too," I said.

Thomas looked at me for a moment.

"I have many wonderful things to tell you

about your father. Would you want to hear them sometime?"

I already knew wonderful things about my father. What would I learn from one of my father's favorite patients, even if he was a nut case?

A cold feeling comes over me as I think that.

I had said "nut case" to my father once, and never ever again. He had made me sit down, and he talked to me about the dignity of people.

"Be thoughtful. Be smart."

He had taken my hand so I wouldn't

think he was angry with me.

"Be kind."

It was almost as if my father was there, looking at me with his serious look.

I remembered my father's kindness to Thomas.

"Yes," I said at last. "I'll talk to you, Thomas."

"I'll call you once a week for two minutes," Thomas said. "I don't want to impose. Two minutes only."

He held up two fingers.

I nodded.

"Day and time?"

"Six fifty Monday evenings," I said. "My night to fix dinner."

Thomas nodded.

"Do you think my father would mind?" I asked.

"No. He wouldn't mind," said Thomas.

And then he walked away.

And every Monday at 6:50 I would talk to Thomas.

I watched him walk down the street.

I opened the envelope.

Inside was a folded piece of paper.

Thomas had written two sentences.

DR. O'BRIEN WAS MY HERO.

HE TAUGHT ME OFTEN THE

TRUTH IS JUST BEHIND A DOOR.

THOMAS

My mind flashes back to something I haven't thought of for a long time. It was when I was five.

"What's real and what isn't real?" I ask my father.

My father peers at me.

"Open the window and maybe you'll know," he says.

"Which window?"

My father taps me on my head.

"That window," he says.

When I looked down the street, Thomas was gone. I read the note again.

Thomas didn't sound much like a nut case.

Maybe just a *bit* of a nut case.

I sighed.

Like the rest of us.

"Play basketball!" my father's handwritten note had said to us.

In the late darkness, with only moonlight, we played basketball in the driveway. No one talked. My mother took off her good shoes and played barefoot.

I passed the basketball to Finn, who tried a jump shot but missed. It hit the rim, and my mother took it and made one of her perfect jump shots.

Duke came out to stand on his lawn, watching us.

Without thinking about what I was doing, I passed the basketball to Duke. He was not a player.

But Duke, from his grassy side yard, did something that surprised us all. He took a breath and, in perfect form, made a long, arching shot that whispered into the basket. *Swish.*

We all turned to stare at Duke.

"Declan taught me that at night," he said simply. "Many nights."

In the moonlight there were tears on his cheeks.

CHAPTER 3

Words

Days moved slowly. Nights, too.

Every night my mother put Finn to bed before she went to her room to study.

Every night Finn came into my room, dragging his quilt, to curl up next to me.

Sometimes he cried in his sleep.

Trying to make things better for him was like trying to wind a tangled ball of yarn.

My father could fix this. *But my father was the problem.*

My mother was here, but not yet here in the old way. But she was trying. She sat us down at the table.

"I am thinking of putting my work off until next summer—my writing and classes. Then I can be here with you. We will spend this summer together."

Finn didn't say anything. He looked over at me.

"I'll be here all summer," I said.

My voice sounded far away, as if it wasn't me talking.

"Fiona will take care of me," Finn said quickly.

Mother kissed us both on the forehead.

"We'll give it a try," she said.

And that was how Finn made me his summer mother.

It was my night to cook. Luke opened the screen door and sat at the table.

"Nice meatballs," he said admiringly.

"Yep. I am the meatball queen. I have to find something else to cook."

I put the rolled-up meatballs in a pan of oil.

"Is that all you have to say?" I asked Luke.

"Yes," said Luke. "Where's Finn?"

I shook my head.

"Upstairs being sad," I said, and suddenly my eyes filled with tears.

That happened those days when I didn't expect it.

Luke nodded. He turned and ran up the stairs and knocked at Finn's bedroom door.

In a while he was back.

He didn't say anything. He tapped my head the way my father had. When I looked up from stirring meatballs in the pan, Luke was gone.

The phone rang. I looked up at the clock. It was 6:50. *I'd forgotten.*

The phone rang again.

"Hello."

"Hello, Fiona. Is this a good time?"

"Yes."

"How are you?"

"I'm fine, but feeling kind of alone."

"I once said that to your father. 'I don't want to be alone!'

"'But Thomas,' he said. 'You're always alone.'"

I thought for a moment.

"It's Finn who is the most sad and alone. He's not talking."

"I remembered saying to your father, 'You're not talking very much.' And your father said, 'I don't talk unless I have something to say.'"

I thought of Luke, a little like my father.

Not many words, but words that meant something.

And now Finn was not talking.

"Maybe Finn doesn't know what he wants to say yet. Maybe you need to find something or someone who has been left alone for Finn to help," said Thomas.

"Like what?"

"You'll know," said Thomas. "Maybe whatever it is will make *you* feel better as well."

I was quiet.

"Fiona?"

"Yes?"

"I'll call you next week."

"Good-bye, Thomas."

"Good-bye, Fiona."

I hung up.

I wrote a note on a slip of paper:

Find something to help Finn.

When I turned around, Finn was sitting at the table.

"I can't stop hating the woman who let her child run out in front of Dad's car," said Finn bluntly. "I can't!"

I sat down next to Finn and put my arm around him.

"We're going to find something to help you. And help me," I said.

"What is it?"

"I don't know. But we'll find it. Say you

believe me. Finn?"

Finn, his face pale, leaned his head on my shoulder.

"I believe you, Fiona," he said very softly.

It was after dinner, Finn gone to bed, my mother studying in her room. I wiped the counters clean with a cloth. I put the dishes away.

The screen door opened and slapped shut. I jumped.

"Fiona! I have found something to help Finn!"

"Luke? It's dark outside."

"I know that," said Luke.

"I found this note of yours on the counter," said Luke. "I was here, and no one was in the kitchen."

Luke held up a printed paper.

"I found this at the post office!"

He read it to me.

"'Volunteers wanted to spend time with abandoned dogs. They need company. They love children. They will love *you*. You can read or talk to them. Spend as much time as you can.'"

So many words from Luke for a change.

"It's at the shelter three blocks away! We can walk there!"

"We?"

Luke shrugged.

"I read the note. And read between the lines," he said. "Your father told me there was often something left unsaid, but it was there. Between the lines."

I stared at Luke.

Those were the most words I'd ever heard Luke say.

When he went out through the screen door, I knew he had found something for Finn.

And he had left all those words for me.

When I went up the stairs to bed, I looked in Finn's room. The desk lamp was on. Finn was sleeping.

Before I turned off the light I saw dozens

of folded papers scattered across his desk. I opened one. Then another.

All notes to Finn from Luke.

Finn,

Let's go fishing next week. I have a fishing pole for you.

Luke

I didn't read any of the other notes. They were for Finn.

I left the light on. I left the notes where they were.

Luke had not only left words for me. He had left them for Finn, too.

CHAPTER 4

Emma

When I got up in the morning, my mother had already gone to class. Luke was sitting in the kitchen, eating cereal. Finn was next to him, eating toast and jam.

"Have you moved in?" I asked Luke.

"In a way," said Luke. "I called the dog shelter, and we'll go today to volunteer. I told Finn."

"I have my books," said Finn. "To read to the dogs."

I could tell he had a question to ask.

"Will this be fun?" he asked Luke.

Luke looked quickly at me. "I don't know if it will be *fun*, Finn. But it will make some sad dog happier," said Luke.

Finn nodded.

What Luke said could have been said by my father.

Finn opened the book at the top of his pile.

"Do you think one of the dogs will like *The Year at Maple Hill Farm*?" he asked.

My father had given Finn that book for a long-ago birthday. It was Finn's favorite. He

35

loved the passing of seasons and how the animals lived.

I couldn't think of an answer.

But Luke had one.

"Yes. But mostly the dogs will like *you*," he said. "Get a bag for your books. We have to go soon."

Finn ran upstairs.

"I haven't had breakfast," I said.

Luke handed me a piece of Finn's toast and jam. I looked sideways at him, about to say something about his notes to Finn. But I didn't.

Those words belonged to them.

* * *

When we opened the door to the dog shelter we were surrounded by happy dogs. Little dogs ran out to be petted. A refined poodle looked over the counter.

"Thank you for coming!" said a woman. "I'm Martha, and some of these happy dogs are only here for a time while their families are on vacation. They miss them, but not too much! We board some dogs. We rescue some dogs."

The poodle came out from behind the counter and walked up to Finn. He grinned.

"Ah, Jenny likes you. She is our calm and rather relaxed rescue dog. She has the run of the place. She doesn't go up to everyone, though. I can tell you'll be good with the dogs."

She opened the door and we went into a room that was quiet.

"The dogs you will see in the rescue room don't have homes anymore."

There were two children sitting on pillows reading books or talking to dogs in their pens.

"Penny is reading to Mindy," said Martha. "And Joe is telling his own story to Marco."

When Marco heard his name, he looked up and wagged his tail.

We heard Penny's soft voice.

"In the great green room
There was a telephone

And a red balloon

And a picture of—

The cow jumping over the moon."

Several dogs came up to look at us.

There were soft beds in their pens, and water bowls and food dishes, stuffed toys, and chew bones.

"This is Betty. She likes people already. And Billy."

"Are they all friendly?" asked Luke.

"Pretty much. Sometimes we put them together for dog company, and for walks. Except for one who doesn't seem to respond to anyone as hard as we try."

Finn sat down on a pillow in front of a pen.

"This one," said Finn.

Inside was a medium-sized, smooth-coated brown dog, facing away from us, staring at the back wall.

Martha looked at us and shrugged.

"That's Emma. Her owner died, and his relatives brought her here. They live far away and couldn't take care of her. All she does is stare at the back wall. Her owner was a musician. He taught somewhere in town. That's all I know."

"I choose Emma," said Finn.

I touched Martha's arm and whispered.

"Finn's father, *our* father, died recently."

Martha nodded.

"Then he will know just how Emma feels," she said. "What's your brother's name?"

"Finn."

"Finn, we're going out to the office to set up a schedule. Emma may do better for you if there aren't all of us here."

Finn nodded and began reading in a soft voice.

"This is a book about farm animals,

And what happens during one year on a farm. . . .

Animals don't know there is such a thing as a year,

But they do know about seasons.
Animals know when the cold will come,
And they grow heavy overcoats."

On the way out I saw the other dogs were at the front of their pens, either sitting or lying down and listening to Finn's voice. Or Penny's voice. Or the story Joe told.

"Once there was a black dog—like you—
who had a job. He herded all the people of
his house to bed at night—the father, the
mother, the children, and the cat. Then,
when they were sleeping he emptied every
wastebasket in the house, leaving tissues on
the floors as morning wakeup gifts for them."

* * *

In the office, still filled with staff people and dogs, we signed up to come four days a week.

Martha looked at my name.

"Are you Declan O'Brien's daughter?"

"Yes."

She took a breath and leaned on the counter.

"I'm so sorry. He was a great man. He once helped me with my son."

"Thank you."

She handed me a leash.

"Want to take Jenny for a walk while you wait for Finn?"

"Sure."

"You can take Char, the lively girl," said Martha, handing another leash to Luke.

And we went out the door and across the grassy lawn.

"Your father is everywhere, isn't he?" said Luke.

"Yes."

"There's nothing bad about that, Fiona," said Luke.

I burst into tears. And Jenny, alarmed at the sound, nosed me gently.

Char scampered around Luke's legs, and he untangled her more than once.

We walked saying nothing, Jenny looking up at me every so often.

When we returned and opened the door,

Martha beckoned to us.

"Penny and Joe have left. It's Finn by himself."

Two staff members stood at the open door to where Finn was still sitting cross-legged, reading.

> *"Dogs speak words*
> *But only poets*
> *And children*
> *Hear"*

Finn took a breath and turned a page.

> *"Lost and Found*
> *"I found the boy at dusk.*

"The blizzard was fierce, and it would soon be dark.

"I could barely see him with the snow blowing sideways. He stood at the edge of the icy pond, shivering."

Martha pointed. Emma was partway down the pen, sitting very still, looking at Finn. *Listening to Finn.*

"That's never happened before," she whispered. "Never in the time that Emma has been here."

We left the open doorway so we wouldn't disturb Finn and Emma.

"Never," Martha said again.

We waited until finally Finn came out,

46

carrying his bag of books.

"Emma liked *my book*!" said Finn. "May I come again tomorrow?" he asked. "I can walk here on my own."

"Of course!" said Martha with great happiness. "You can move in if you want."

"I'll think about that," said Finn.

"And please leave *some* of your books with us. We can try reading one to her."

Finn turned to me.

"I need more books!" he said, his voice, for the first time in a while, full of light.

CHAPTER 5

Turnabout

My mother came home from class, plunking her books on the table. I smiled at her.

"The schoolgirl returns," I said.

"You sound like me," said my mother.

"I know."

She sat down at the table.

"I have something to tell you," I said.

"Me, too," she said. "Something I forgot to

tell you. You first."

"Thomas, the nut case, calls me once a week for two minutes."

"That's the very thing I meant to tell you. He called me to ask if I minded. He didn't want to do anything improper."

"Thomas is never improper," I said.

"No, he is not," said my mother. "And stop calling him a nut case."

"Nut case is just a description," I said.

"Not for Thomas," said my mother firmly. "I've known Thomas for years. He had parents who didn't know how to be parents. They were both depressed, and they expected Thomas to make them happy. He was their only child."

"That's terrible," I said.

"It is. I imagine your father never heard you call any of the people he helped nut cases, did he?"

"Only once," I said. "And never again to him."

"And never again to me either," said my mother. "You hear?"

I nodded.

"Claire!" said Finn, coming into the kitchen. "I read to a sad dog today at the shelter. I was good at it."

My mother smiled. Finn was experimenting with calling my mother by her first name.

"I bet you were," she said.

"I need more books for Emma," said Finn.

"I vote for *Mr. Rabbit and the Lovely Present*," said my mother. "A favorite of mine."

"Good idea," said Finn, running upstairs. "There's nothing better than making a dog happy!" he called.

"And there's nothing better than making a *boy* happy," said my mother to no one in particular. She had one of her faraway looks.

It was almost like I wasn't there anymore.

I didn't mind.

Sometimes I was inside my own head, too.

"I'm here with new books," Finn told Martha the moment he opened the door to the shelter.

"I see that," said Martha.

"*Mr. Rabbit and the Lovely Present*," said Finn,

waving the book. "Did you read to Emma?"

"We did," said Martha, "but she turned her head around only once as if to say, 'Where's the boy?'"

"The boy is here, Emma," called Finn.

"Hi, Joe. Hi, Penny," he said as he disappeared into the rescue room.

"I'll walk Jenny," I said.

Jenny came over to me, hearing her name.

There was a wildly leaping little dog at Martha's feet.

Martha handed Luke a leash.

"Will you please calm Lulu down with a walk outside?"

"I will," said Luke. "Lulu, sit," he commanded.

Lulu sat.

Martha grinned.

"I think the children should take over the shelter," she said.

"The dogs already have," said Luke, making Martha laugh.

"I like walking Jenny," I said. "She's with me whether I'm happy or sad."

Martha smiled.

"Yes, Jenny has a bit of the mind reader in her. She'll make someone very happy, whoever adopts her. Whoever *she* chooses, of course," added Martha.

She looked at me for a moment.

"The truth is that we know the dogs need people. But people need the dogs even more sometimes. To teach people how good they really can be. I call it turnabout."

I thought about Finn and Emma—helping each other.

When I went outside with Jenny and found Luke with Lulu, I saw the bumper sticker on Martha's car.

I pointed it out to Luke.

BE THE PERSON YOUR DOG THINKS YOU ARE.

Monday night. Meatball night. Luke was not here to admire my meatballs. He was not here to sound like my father. He had gone out to dinner with Duke and Daisy. Finn was upstairs, his door open. He was humming.

Actually humming.

The phone rang. I turned the heat down under the pan of meatballs.

"Hello?"

"Hello, Fiona."

"Thomas, I have a confession to make to you."

"What is that?"

"I called you a nut case before I found out you weren't," I said.

Thomas laughed.

"So I'm cured?"

I don't remember ever hearing Thomas laugh before. Never on the phone. Never when I was little and he came to our house.

"I have called myself the same," he said.

"Do not do that," I said. "My mother said it was wrong, and my father would not like it."

"I have a confession, too. I called your mother to make sure it was proper to call you."

"I know."

"Your mother is a kind woman. Once when I came to your house for comfort, your little brother started to cry. I thought maybe it was my fault. I said to her, 'Please find me a place to be where I don't hurt anyone's feelings.' And she took me up to your father's office until he came and sent me home. Always with gentleness."

I thought about my mother knowing more

than I did about most everything. I thought about Thomas's parents, who wished for him to make their lives right.

"Fiona?"

"Yes?"

"I'll call you next week."

"Good-bye, Thomas."

"Good-bye, Fiona."

I was sorry to hang up. I hadn't told Thomas about Emma and Finn. I hadn't asked him if he had a pet. I heard Martha's words in my head. Sometimes people needed dogs to teach the people how good they can be.

CHAPTER 6

Always the Sun

When Luke walked into the kitchen as he did every morning, I was the only one there.

"You alone," he said, surprised.

"Just me," I said. "My mother has gone to class. Finn's sleeping."

"I have a question," I said.

"So early?" said Luke, smiling a bit.

"You're an only child. Do your parents expect you to make everything perfect for them?"

Luke laughed a lot.

"Think of Daisy and Duke, Fiona. Do you believe they really need me to keep them happy?"

That was true. Duke was a large, husky writer who looked like a wrestler but who wrote tender, sweet words about love and life. Daisy was a biologist and knew many gruesome and interesting facts about snakes, the surprising behavior of crows, and the digestive habits of llamas.

"I guess you're right. They're happy without

depending on you."

"Why this question?" asked Luke.

I thought a moment.

"Well, one of my father's patients I've known for a long time calls me once a week to tell me about my father."

Luke nodded.

"Six fifty, right?" said Luke. "Mondays."

My mouth opened. Did Luke know *everything*?

"I was coming into the kitchen one evening and knew you were having a private talk," said Luke. "I . . ."

"Read between the lines," we said at the same time.

It was quiet.

"Thomas's parents expected their only child to make their sad lives right. To fix everything."

"That's why Thomas grew up sad," said Luke.

"He should have had a father and mother like yours and mine," I said, feeling the sudden jolt of who I was missing.

"But Thomas brings your father back to you in a way," said Luke. "My father once wrote me a poem about being a father. It ended with the line 'And I'm the light that will never go out.'"

I stared at Luke.

"You're not going to cry, are you?" he asked.

I shook my head.

"No."

I shook my head again.

"What?" asked Luke.

"We just have to keep the light burning for Finn," I said softly.

"We are, Fiona," said Luke. "You are. And Emma will."

Luke peered at me the same way my father used to peer at me.

"You never know. Someone may come along to help keep the light on for Finn."

"You sound like my father," I said.

He nodded.

"Now you can cry," he said.

And I did.

* * *

"I have something new for Emma," said Finn as he, Luke, and I walked to the shelter.

"New books?" asked Luke.

"Music," said Finn. "Martha said Emma's owner was a musician. He must have played music. Wouldn't Emma miss music?"

"How do you know all this?" I asked.

"I talk to Martha. And I listen."

Luke smiled at me over Finn's head.

"Emma will like music. I remember our parents singing to us when we were little," I said.

Finn laughed. I stopped on the sidewalk and stared at him as he and Luke walked ahead. He hadn't laughed for such a long time. I'd forgotten the sound.

"What?" said Finn, looking back at me.

"Why are you laughing?" I asked Finn.

"I'm laughing because Mother can't sing. She's tone-deaf. You remember wrong."

Finn was right. It was my father. When we played basketball, he sang. *And he sang when he cooked his runny eggs.*

I started walking again. I took Finn's hand and walked on to the shelter.

I wonder why Finn remembers better than I do.

"Maybe it is because it is safer for you to forget right now," said Luke.

I realized I'd spoken out loud.

And Luke, as always, had answered me.

* * *

There was bedlam at the shelter, and Finn disappeared inside the rescue room.

"Penny is reading a poem," said Martha.

I listened.

> *"The cow*
> *Coming*
> *Across the grass*
> *Moves*
> *Like a mountain*
> *Toward us"*

Then Joe began a very energetic version of *Where the Wild Things Are.*

"Wild thing!" Joe called over and over again.

Marco and Billy began barking. I had never heard barking in the rescue room before. It was usually so sadly quiet.

"I need Jenny," I said to Martha.

Martha nodded and looked at Luke.

"I'll take Lulu if she's here. We have come to an understanding."

Martha laughed.

Luke and I went out the door, up and down the lawns, across the street to a park. We sat on a bench, and Jenny sat close, looking up at me. I patted her.

Lulu jumped up on the bench and lay down

next to Luke. It was peaceful.

"Maybe Thomas should have a dog," I said in the quiet.

"You can tell him that tonight when he calls," Luke said.

"Meatball night already? So soon?"

"Yes."

Jenny nosed my hand as if to say, "It's all right. It's all right."

We got up and walked back through the park, across the shelter lawn, and when we opened the door, Martha was grinning at us.

The rescue room door was ajar.

Music was playing. It was Finn's small tape deck. It was an orchestra playing "Dona Nobis

Pacem." My father's song.

I pushed the door open and looked in. Joe and Penny were sitting still. The dogs were listening to Finn's music. I walked in, trying to be quiet. When I came closer, Finn looked up at me and smiled.

Emma sat far closer to Finn, much closer than she'd ever been.

She looked up and saw me. I was very still, afraid I'd scare her. But I didn't. She sat there, looking and listening. She looked at me, then back at Finn, as if assuring herself that Finn and I were family. We were safe.

And then she lay down, listening to the music. Finn and Emma and I didn't move. We didn't move until the music ended.

Finn got up. "I'll be back," he whispered to Emma.

We walked out past Penny and Joe, and when I looked back, Emma was still there.

Emma had come away from the wall.

My meatballs were sizzling.

The phone rang.

"Hello?"

"Hello, Fiona."

"Hello, Thomas."

"How are you? How is Finn?"

"My friend Luke found something for Finn. He is working with a shelter dog whose owner died."

"That's a good thing."

"Luke is an only child, like you. His father once wrote him a poem about being a father. The last line was 'And I'm the light that will never go out.'"

Thomas sighed.

"Your father once said the same thing to me. He said, 'There'll always be the sun. Always the sun.' It's a light that never goes out."

"Do you have a dog, Thomas? The shelter woman says that people sometimes need dogs to teach them how good they are."

"I have a cat," said Thomas.

"Then the cat will let you know how good you are," I said.

I could almost feel Thomas smile through the phone.

"My cat is a hisser, a talker, and a scratcher. I rescued him off the streets."

"See? You are really, really good!"

"Maybe you're right."

"Today Finn played 'Dona Nobis Pacem' for Emma the dog. She moved closer to him."

"Your father loved music. I'm a singer, and he always said, 'Keep on singing!'"

"Sometimes I forget things about him."

"Memories are good. At least your father thought so. 'Maybe the reason you and I are here is to collect memories,' he once said."

"Is that what we're doing?" I asked.

"Yes. It is what we're doing. I'll call you again next week, Fiona."

"Good-bye, Thomas."

"Good-bye, Fiona."

I hung up.

Collecting memories.

I stirred the meatballs in the pan.

And suddenly I remembered my father telling me that *dona nobis pacem* was Latin for "grant us peace."

"What's better than that?" he says.
"Peace. Besides, it annoys your mother when I sing it to her when we're playing

tense competitive basketball."

We both laugh.

How was it I'd forgotten that? It had been lost. But it wasn't anymore.

I was collecting memories.

CHAPTER 7

Comfort

My mother and Finn and I sat in the kitchen after dinner. I could hear the katydid sounds outside, like dusk music.

My father holds up his finger when he hears that sound. "Summer song," he says.

"What?" asked my mother, seeing the look on my face.

"That sound."

"He liked it. *'Katydid, Katydidn't,'*" my mother said.

"He knew the songs of the oriole, the cardinal, the veery by the river, and the high call of the sharp-shinned hawk," said Finn, ticking them off on his fingers.

My mother and I looked at each other, surprised. Finn was beginning to talk as much as Luke was these days.

"You remembered all that," said my mother.

"And I listened. Like Emma," said Finn. "She liked 'Dona Nobis Pacem' when I played the tape for her."

"Your father's song. He used to sing it to me in a fierce basketball game so I'd get

75

distracted," said my mother. "Imagine the nerve of him singing a gentle song meaning 'grant us peace' when I was trying to beat him up in basketball."

Finn and I grinned at each other, remembered it working from time to time.

"You know, Finn, maybe you should sing to Emma. You have a beautiful voice, and I think animals react to voices," said my mother.

"Do dogs like music?" I asked.

She shrugged. "Maybe, maybe not," she said. "I mostly know about young children. Not dogs. Young children respond to singing."

"Maybe dogs and young children are alike," Finn said with his thoughtful look. He peered at my mother.

"Right now you look just like your father," she said softly.

She was right. My father's direct and thoughtful look as if he was just discovering the thing he'd say next.

"So maybe it is not the stories I've been reading," said Finn. "Maybe it's my *voice* that Emma likes."

"Thomas said Father once told him, 'Keep on singing,'" I said.

"Who is Thomas?" asked Finn.

"A very wise friend of Father's," I said.

My mother smiled.

It was quiet then in the kitchen.

"Is there a music school in town?" asked Finn idly.

"Well, there is the Chance Conservatory," said my mother. "Over on West Avenue, across the park from the shelter."

Finn looked up as if startled.

"Chance? Is that the name?" asked Finn.

"Why are you asking?" said my mother.

"Just wondering," he said.

I remember my father once watching Finn look out the window in winter as the snow fell.

"What are you doing?" my father asks.

"Just wondering," Finn says.

"Just wondering is good," my father says.

78

"Actually, I'm making a plan," said Finn. "Emma's owner who died was named David Chance. Martha told me."

"Shall I ask what the plan is?" I said.

"No," said Finn.

The only sounds were the katydids' steady soft song as dusk turned into night.

Katydid, Katydidn't.

Katydid, Katydidn't.

Katydid, Katydidn't.

Memories.

At the shelter Finn went right into the rescue room as if he lived there now.

"Joe and Penny are not here today," said Martha. "It's pretty quiet in the rescue room."

Jenny came right over, looking up at me. I knelt down and hugged her.

I thought of Finn's words about the dogs liking the sound of a voice.

"I'm fine, Jenny. Let's go for a walk."

Martha handed me the leash across the counter.

"You're talking to her now," she said.

I stared at her. Was it *me* who hadn't been talking?

Martha nodded as if she had heard my thoughts.

"Jenny likes the sound of your voice."

"Sometimes she acts as if *I* need *her*," I said.

"Instead of the other way around."

"Maybe you do."

"Turnabout?" I asked.

"Turnabout," said Martha.

I hooked the leash to Jenny's collar.

"Luke will be coming in a while," I said. "Give him some impossible dog, will you?"

Martha grinned.

"I know just the perfect one!"

Martha opened the door to the rescue room, and we heard the sweet, clear voice of Finn singing "Hush, Little Baby." I stood still, my heart beating faster. I remembered the words.

Hush little baby, don't say a word,
Papa's gonna buy you a mockingbird.

And if that mockingbird won't sing,
Papa's gonna buy you a diamond ring.

My father sang it to us at night. I hadn't heard it in a long time. But I remembered every word of it.

I opened the door, and Jenny and I walked out into the sunlight. We crossed the lawn and went over the road to the park.

"You're the best girl, Jenny," I said.

She shook her head happily, making me smile.

"We'll sit on this bench."

I sat, and Jenny leaned against me, looking for other dogs. She lifted her nose, sniffing the air.

I took a dog treat from my pocket and held it out for her. She didn't move. Finally, after a minute, she sat.

"Oh, did someone once ask you to sit for a treat?"

For the first time I thought about Jenny, left behind at the shelter. She was always friendly and serene. I had thought so much of Emma and her sadness.

But Jenny had been left, too.

"Wait! Stop! Sit!"

I looked up and saw Luke coming with a very large dog pulling him across the street.

Jenny woofed happily and stood, wagging her tail.

The very large dog pulled Luke over to our

bench. I burst out laughing as Luke fell next to me.

"This dog is impossible!" he said, out of breath.

"Martha told me she had the perfect dog for you. What kind of dog is it?"

Luke shook his head as Jenny and the impossible dog nosed each other.

"My father raised a miniature pony for 4-H the size of this dog," said Luke. "This dog's name is Ralph."

"Hello, Ralph," I said, and Ralph came over to me, his huge head next to mine, sniffing my eyes. His breath was warm as he explored my face.

"Where's Finn?" asked Luke.

"He's singing to Emma. He thinks maybe it isn't the *stories* that she likes, but his voice that comforts her. So he's singing."

Luke smiled.

"Finn is doing much better," he said.

I nodded.

"But he still comes to curl up in my bed at night. And he cries in his sleep."

"He's thinking about the accident. And wanting to find someone to blame," said Luke.

I sighed.

Jenny nosed my hand.

"She's comforting you," said Luke.

"Yes. Jenny comforts me."

I stroked Jenny's head.

"What will be Finn's comfort? He spends

his time comforting Emma. But what will comfort him?"

Luke shook his head.

"Maybe helping Emma *is* Finn's comfort," he said.

Jenny put her head in my lap.

Comfort.

CHAPTER 8

Let It Float
down the River

My father once told me, "Life sometimes happens with events falling over each other like tumbleweeds in a prairie wind. Tumbleweed! Like my music."

L ater I would think of his words, even though I had never seen tumbleweeds.

Luke, Finn, and I were in the kitchen, as always. I rolled the meatballs for the pasta sauce. It was late afternoon.

"Mother's here," said Finn, surprised. He sat at the table with a pile of books. "I just heard her car in the driveway."

I looked out and saw another car stop at the curb.

"But this is her late night," I said.

A woman got out of the car. She opened the backseat door and unbuckled a small child from a car seat. I'd never seen the woman or the child before.

And then I knew.

I knew as my mother, the woman, and the child came up the steps together.

It's the woman and child from my father's accident. I knew.

I went over to stand behind Finn as he looked through his books.

When Luke saw I was protecting Finn, he knew, too.

My mother opened the door and smiled at us all.

"Oh good, everyone's here."

The woman came in, holding her little boy's hand.

"Should I go home?" asked Luke.

My mother shook her head.

"No, you're family, Luke. Please stay. This is Mrs. Clark."

"Jessie," the woman said. "And this is Noah. He's only two and doesn't speak very much."

"Two," said Noah.

We all smiled, except for Finn.

"I'm Fiona and my friend Luke."

Jessie nodded.

"And this is my brother, Finn."

"Finn," said Noah, happy with the word.

"Jessie's here because she was there at your father's accident. She wanted to tell you what happened," said my mother.

Jessie had a pale face surrounded by pale hair.

"I wanted to tell you what a hero your father was," said Jessie.

Finn started to get up, but I put my hand on his shoulder.

"Wait," I said softly. "Just wait."

"I was walking with Noah when some children threw a ball into the road, and a dog started to run after it, its leash trailing. Cars were coming, and I tried to grab the leash and still hang on to Noah. Noah's hand slipped out of mine, and he ran after the dog."

She stopped and sighed.

"I couldn't grab the dog's leash."

Her eyes filled with tears.

"And I fell before I could grab Noah," she said. "Your father avoided hitting Noah and the dog. And me. He was a hero."

She sighed again. "I've been thinking about this for a long time."

Noah wandered over to Finn and touched

Finn's hand that was resting on a book.

"Finn," he said in his small voice.

It was quiet in the room. And then Finn looked up at Jessie.

"I've been thinking about this for a long time, too," said Finn.

Jessie nodded. "I know."

"But seeing you and hearing your words has changed the way I think of you."

Jessie sat down in a chair.

"I can't blame you anymore," said Finn softly. "I can't blame Noah."

He paused, as if looking for the words. "And I can't blame my father."

He opened the book *The Year at Maple Hill*

Farm and showed it to Noah. He began to read.

"*June is the first month of summer. The farm pond is overflowing. Horses eat grass. Geese eat grass. Cows and sheep and goats eat grass.*"

Noah pointed.

"Cow," he said.

"Horse," said Finn.

"Horse," repeated Noah.

"It *looks* like a cow," said Finn.

Noah smiled.

"Cow," he repeated with a smile, as if this

93

was a joke between the two of them.

Finn turned some pages.

"August is the last summer month. The sky is blue. The sun shines. . . .

"Almost asleep in a puddle of dust, a dog will still wag his tail as you walk by."

I saw tears in my mother's eyes. Tears came down Jessie's face. There must have been tears in Finn's eyes, too, because Noah reached up to touch them.

But Finn kept reading to Noah.

The same way Finn kept reading to Emma.

"Duck," said Noah, pointing.

"Goose," said Finn.

Noah grinned at the word.

"Goooosse," he said, stretching out the word.

My mother had gone back to class. Jessie and Noah had gone.

Luke and I were quiet, as if we had no words left in us for now.

"You once said that someone might come along to help keep the light on for Finn," I said to Luke.

Luke nodded. He tapped me on the head and opened the screen door. And I watched him walk across the lawn to his house.

Finn sat at the table, looking at *The Year at*

Maple Hill Farm. His favorite book when he was little.

"Are you all right?" I asked, getting out the dinner dishes and the frying pan.

Finn nodded. "I liked Jessie," he said. "She was brave."

"Kind of a hero," I said.

He looked up at me.

"There are many heroes," he said in a voice almost as small as Noah's small voice.

The phone rang. Finn got up and answered. "Hello?"

The moment I heard him say hello, I remembered it was Thomas.

"No, this is Finn. Fiona is cooking."

He was quiet.

"Oh, my father's friend."

Finn listened.

"Yes. The woman who was at my father's accident came today. I can't blame her anymore. I can't blame her little boy. And I can't blame my father," said Finn.

Finn listened and nodded. "I'll remember."

There was a pause, and I knew Thomas was saying good-bye.

"Good-bye, Thomas."

Finn hung up the phone.

"Thomas said he'll call you next week."

I waited, not wanting my words to get in the way.

"He said our father once told him he could let many bad feelings 'float down the river on a little boat.' The things you can't solve," said Finn.

I remembered a time my father had said the same to me.

I am in second grade, and my friend Millie is mean to me. I am complaining to my father.

"Did Millie say she was sorry?" he asks me.

"She did."

"Are you friends again?"

"Yes."

"Well then, let the whole thing float down the river on a little boat. Good-bye!"

And I do.

And that night, for the first time since the accident, Finn slept in his own bed all night.

He didn't cry in his sleep.

Emma had come away from the wall.

Finn had let some of his bad feelings float down the river on a little boat.

CHAPTER 9

Dona Nobis Pacem

When I woke in the morning it was late. I jumped out of bed and went to Finn's room. His bed was made.

His bed was made?!

I couldn't remember when Finn had last made his bed.

My mother's room was empty, her books gone.

I hurried downstairs. Luke sat in the kitchen

calmly eating vanilla Swiss almond ice cream.

"Where did you find that?!"

"In the basement freezer," said Luke. "Your mother keeps a stash there."

"Where is Finn? We're late!"

Luke held up a handwritten note and gave it to me.

"Finn left an hour ago," said Luke.

Today is the day.
Today I sing.
Today I find Emma's true home.
                                        Finn

"I found it here on the table," said Luke.

I sat down.

"Finn said he had a plan but wouldn't tell me. What does he mean 'true home'? I thought Finn might want to adopt Emma himself."

Luke shook his head.

I reached over and took his ice cream bowl and spoon and began eating.

"I think we should go," said Luke.

"I'm ready," I said.

"You have your pajamas on," said Luke.

"I don't care."

"They're plaid. You never wear plaid."

I grabbed Luke's arm, and we started off to the shelter.

When we opened the door, Martha pointed.

"Wild pants," she said.

"I told you," said Luke.

Dogs swarmed around us, wagging their tails.

"Where's Finn?" I said. "He left before I got up this morning."

Martha pointed to the door, open an inch. "He's been singing his sweet song in his sweet voice for an hour. And something amazing has happened. He has taught the song, a canon, to Penny and Joe. They don't get it right sometimes, but they're working at it. You'd better go in to see for yourself."

Luke and I went slowly through the door.

Voices surrounded us—the high, sure

103

voices singing in unison. Sometimes they sang together, sometimes in parts that blended.

"Dona nobis pacem, pacem.

Dona nobis pacem."

The staff members were there. All the dogs were listening. Jenny came over to see me.

"I'm here, Jenny," I whispered. "I'm here."

We walked closer as Finn and Penny and Joe kept singing. Emma didn't even look up at us.

She moved closer and closer. Then she turned back for a second and picked up her blue stuffed toy. Finn still sang.

"Dona nobis pacem, pacem.

Dona nobis pacem."

Emma came up to where Finn sat. And she pushed her toy through a space in the pen. A gift for Finn.

He reached out and touched her nose. She licked his hand.

And still they sang.

They sang my father's song. The music that sounded like tumbleweeds blowing in a prairie wind.

Martha came to stand next to me. She held a leash.

When Finn and Penny and Joe finished the

song, Finn still stroked Emma's face through the pen.

And I knew that the leash Martha carried was for Emma. Emma was going for a walk with Finn.

Finn came out of the rescue room.

Martha handed the leash to him. "Do you want me to help you?"

Finn shook his head.

"I know how to open her door. I've done it before," he confessed as he went back into the rescue room.

Martha handed me Jenny's leash. "Emma may be frightened or skittish," said Martha.

"I'll walk with them without a dog today," said Luke.

"You mean you don't want some new troublesome dog?" asked Martha with a sly look. "I have two small, fluffy dogs named Betty and Bitts. They tumble all over each other. I can't tell them apart. I don't know if they can either."

"Not today," said Luke with a smile.

And then Finn came out with Emma, who did not look skittish or nervous. She walked next to Finn as if they'd been walking together day after day.

Maybe they had.

"I'll sing to her," said Finn. "And we'll

have a conversation."

"Let me know if Emma has anything interesting to say," said Martha.

And then we went out the door, Jenny nosing Emma, and Emma nosing her back.

Emma wagged her tail.

"Ah, she has a tail!" Luke said softly.

And I realized that we hadn't seen it. Emma, for much of the time, had been a huddled-up body, facing the wall.

"Good girl, Emma," said Finn. Then softer, "Don't talk about her tail. She might be shy about it."

"You taught Penny and Joe 'Dona Nobis Pacem'?" I asked Finn.

"Yes. Father taught me all the parts."

"Where was I, I wonder?" I said.

Finn just smiled.

"Father said it is beautiful when all the parts were sung together. But it is simple enough to sound beautiful even if he sang it all by himself on the basketball court at night. He could hear all the parts in his head."

I stopped walking, remembering.

Finn and Emma stopped, too. Jenny looked up at me.

"What?" asked Luke.

"In my room one night, before I went to sleep, I opened the window. He sang it softly, almost to himself out in the dark. His voice was beautiful."

"Even as he bounced the basketball and

made and missed baskets," said Luke. "I could hear him from my own room."

We walked across the lawn and crossed the street to the park. We walked several paths and were about to sit down on a bench when Emma suddenly straightened and stared at the far end of the park.

"Let's keep walking," said Finn, smiling at me.

I knew what the smile meant. "Finn has a plan," I reminded Luke.

Luke nodded. Jenny looked up at me.

"Keep on walking, Jenny," I said.

I leaned down to hug her. She licked my face.

And then, all of a sudden, Emma began walking faster and wagging her tail. Finn had trouble keeping up with her, and Luke ran up to walk next to him.

Luke put his hand over Finn's to help him. Jenny and I went faster, too. Jenny seemed happy with the fast pace.

And then we came to the other side of the park. Luke helped Finn hold on to Emma. We had never walked this far before.

I looked across the street at a tall brick-and-stone building. Finn saw my look.

"The Chance Conservatory," said Finn.

"Chance," I repeated, suddenly remembering what Martha had told Finn.

111

"The name of Emma's owner," said Finn, nodding.

And we crossed the street, Emma leading, straining at the leash. She wagged her tail and began walking up the steps of the tall building.

"What are we doing?" I asked, Jenny cheerfully running up the steps, following Emma and Finn and Luke.

Emma jumped up on the door of the building.

Finn opened the door, and we all went inside.

There was a great center hall and many doors, and stairs going up.

We could hear music behind every door: violins and cellos behind one, an orchestra behind large double doors, and a choir behind another.

A place of music.

Finn went up to a counter. A woman was working at a computer. She looked up to see Finn there.

"Hi. May I do something for you?"

And then Emma jumped up and looked over the counter, her tail wagging.

The woman rose and almost tripped, standing up to the counter.

"Emma! Oh, Emma!" she said loudly.

The woman opened a door and came out into the big hallway, then sat down on the floor and took Emma in her arms. Emma licked the woman's face, wiggling around like a puppy and ending up on her lap.

"Oh, Emma!" she cried again. Then louder she called, "Richard! Richard!!"

A door opened, and a tall man came out. Behind him a string quartet played on.

"What, Estelle?"

And then he saw Emma. And he let out a yell and sat down next to Estelle. Emma went from lap to lap. He looked at us.

"We thought she was with David's family. We've missed her! Who are you?"

The large door opened, and the singers came out, filing up the hallway.

"Callie! Come see!" called Estelle, still sitting on the floor, where now Jenny licked her face, too.

And Callie was as happy as anyone else to see Emma.

I was about to say something. But Finn spoke.

"She was left at the dog shelter across the park," said Finn. "She was so unhappy. She only looked at the back wall. I volunteered to read and sing to her. She liked music best. And when I sang 'Dona Nobis Pacem,' she came close to me."

"That's what the choir had been learning when Emma was last here!" said Callie.

"It was my father's favorite song," said Finn, his voice softer. "Maybe the song brought her back here."

I could feel tears in my eyes.

Finn took a breath. "She was wondering all along where you were," said Finn. "Now she's found you."

Then Finn burst into tears. Estelle got up and put her arms around Finn.

"You're a hero," she said, which made Finn cry harder. "We'll adopt Emma. All of us. Richard lives here in David's apartment! You've brought her back to us!"

Estelle kept her arms around Finn. She cried, too.

And Emma leaned against the two of them.

As if we were in a dream, Luke and I knew what to do. We went behind the counter to call Martha. Jenny followed. No one noticed us. Children had come out of a music class and run to Emma.

"Emma, Emma!"

Luke dialed the phone on the desk. "Martha? It's Luke. No, no, there's nothing wrong."

Luke shook his head. He couldn't speak. He handed me the phone.

"Martha? It's Fiona."

"What is happening?!"

"Finn has found Emma's true home," I said.

There was silence.

"Martha?"

117

"How could he do that?"

Her voice broke. Martha was crying. Was everyone crying?

"Martha? Emma will be living at the conservatory across the park. The Chance Conservatory."

I waited for Martha to remember what she had told Finn. And she did.

"Chance," she said softly.

"They are overjoyed to see her. They want her. And Martha?"

"What?"

I took a deep breath.

"We're not bringing Emma back to the shelter."

* * *

We closed the big door of the conservatory behind us, leaving Emma in her true home. Finn and Luke and I walked Jenny down the stairs, across the street to the park.

Jenny looked at us all as if to say, "Why aren't you talking?"

I smiled at her and whispered in her ear, "Good girl. What an adventure we had."

She pranced a little at the sound of my whisper. We walked for a while.

"That was quite a plan of yours," Luke said to Finn.

Finn smiled.

"I thought hard for a long time. Father once said to me, 'If it's hard, you're doing good things.'"

No one said anything. We walked silently across the park, back through paths we hadn't walked before until today.

Emma had led us.

CHAPTER 10

Jenny

We walked down the yard to the shelter. "Are you sad a bit? Emma going there instead of home with you?" I asked Finn.

"No. The conservatory is her true home. It is where she is meant to be. Richard ran out to buy her favorite food."

Finn shrugged his shoulders.

"I can visit Emma whenever I want. They told me."

"I'm kind of sad myself," I said.

"Then talk to Jenny," said Finn, making me smile. Finn was smart. Smart like Martha.

When we got to the shelter, a woman was coming out with Lulu on a leash. Lulu was going home.

Lulu pulled on the leash. Luke couldn't help himself.

"Sit, Lulu," he said firmly. Lulu looked up at Luke and sat.

"Oh my," said the woman. "Where have you been all my life?"

"Lulu and I took walks together while you were away. You can do it, I'm sure." We laughed as we went up the steps to the front door.

122

"No," said Luke softly. "She'll never control Lulu. She's not an alpha. Lulu rules."

And when we opened the door, there was my mother! She stood by the counter talking to Martha.

"I called your mother and told her what a great job you did for Emma. She wanted to come to the shelter."

"And did you sing 'Dona Nobis Pacem'?" my mother asked.

"I did. And at the conservatory Callie told me she had been teaching that to the choir when Emma was there," said Finn.

Martha's eyes were red and puffy. She came around the counter and gave Finn a hug.

"I am still going to come to the shelter," said Finn. "Maybe I'll read to Marco. He's a bit shy."

Martha smiled.

"There will *always* be more dogs," she said.

I had unleashed Jenny and hung up the leash.

Jenny surprised me. She walked right up to my mother and sat down, gazing up at her.

"That's Jenny," I said. "I walk her every day."

"And in return Jenny comforts Fiona," said Luke.

My mother sat down on a bench, and Jenny went over to my mother and put her head in my mother's lap.

"Martha and I have noticed that Jenny protects and likes the people who need her," I said.

"So I see," said my mother.

Martha took Jenny's leash off the wall where I'd put it. "Here." She handed me the leash.

"What?"

Martha smiled. "I told you Jenny would choose the people she loved. She chose Finn first, then you. And now she has chosen your mother," she said softly.

And that is how we took Jenny home.

We piled into Mother's car, Jenny in the backseat sitting between Finn and Luke. She licked Finn's face. He was the first she had loved. She tried to sit on Luke's lap and put her head out the window, but that didn't work well.

If a dog could smile, Jenny was smiling.

When we turned into the driveway, Jenny went to the front door, went into the house, and chose my mother's favorite white couch.

"Let her be," said my mother.

Luke laughed.

"This is what Father used to call 'the eternal fitness of things,'" said Finn brightly.

"What?" I said. "What do you know about that?" I asked.

My father had said those words the last time he cooked us runny omelets. I had asked him before he'd rushed out the door.

"Father told me it was the way things are or should be. It is like the seasons in the book *The Year at Maple Hill Farm*. Winter begins, followed by spring, then summer and fall. The animals know it. It is their eternal fitness of things. It is Emma going home to the place she loves. Her true home."

Finn thought a moment.

"Thomas would say it was Jessie coming here to tell us about the accident that was no one's fault," he said.

Jenny walked into the kitchen and Luke put down a food dish.

"And it is Jenny coming here," said Luke.

My mother cried.

127

* * *

It was dusk.

The katydids were beginning their song outside.

Jenny had eaten, explored every room in the house, sniffing the smell of them all. She had gone for two walks, happy when Duke and Daisy came out next door to meet her.

"Oh, maybe there is a dog at the shelter for us, too!" said Daisy, excited.

"So far there is not," said Luke, making Duke laugh.

My mother had gone to class late, leaving us pizza so I didn't have to cook.

The phone rang.

I answered without thinking.

"Hello?"

"Hello, Fiona."

"Hello, Thomas. We just adopted a dog, Jenny."

"Then you will know every day how good you are," said Thomas.

"And Finn found the true home for Emma, the lost dog. Maybe I should sit down and write about all this so I don't forget," I said. "Like a journal."

"Your father once said, 'The only good thing about journals is the date.' I think he meant, when the days pass by, we progress and grow as well. Something to think about."

I was quiet.

"Fiona?"

"Yes?"

"If I was to write a book about your father, it would be titled *Growing Up One Hour at a Time*."

I smiled at this. I knew my father's sessions lasted for an hour each week.

"Or," I said suddenly, "*My Father's Words*."

Thomas was silent for a moment.

"Oh yes," he said softly.

"Oh yes," I repeated.

"I'll call you next week," said Thomas.

"Good-bye, Thomas."

"Good-bye, Fiona."

* * *

That night, when Luke had gone home and we went to bed, Jenny slept with me.

"No," said Finn in the morning. "Jenny slept with me!"

"But she slept with me, too," said my mother.

And she laughed.

My mother laughed again!

Jenny had slept with all of us.

CHAPTER 11

THE CELEBRATION OF EMMA
Music Brought Her Back

We went to the conservatory for the celebration. Many people were there. There were children and two visiting dogs. We didn't know them, but they knew Emma.

Estelle hugged us. So did Richard and Callie.

My mother, Jessie and Noah, Duke and Daisy, Martha and the staff of the shelter were there. Penny and Joe were there, too.

My mother beckoned to Thomas, who came to sit next to her.

Luke and Jenny and I sat up front with Finn.

The orchestra played—the cellos and violins, the viola and bass, the brass and woodwinds—and the child musicians were in the front.

Emma was there, her blue stuffed toy beside her. When the choir began to sing, she saw Finn and brought the toy to him.

Callie, the choir director, turned and directed us along with the beautiful voices of her choir.

We sang.

We all knew the song—our father's favorite.

"Dona nobis pacem, pacem.
Dona nobis pacem."

The music fell around us like tumbleweeds.
Tumbleweeds. Like my father's words.

My father would be happy.

AUTHOR'S NOTE

There are many YouTube performances under the title "Dona Nobis Pacem."

Swedish orchestral arrangement:

www.youtube.com/watch?v=OSdGW_HBrLE

Another is a charming rendition of an entire school performing.

Waring School arrangement:

www.youtube.com/watch?v=v5FZAk497D4

More great books by
PATRICIA MacLACHLAN!

Sarah, Plain and Tall series

HARPER
An Imprint of HarperCollins Publishers

KATHERINE TEGEN BOOKS
An Imprint of HarperCollins Publishers

www.harpercollinschildrens.com